When
ROSA PARKS
Went Fishing

by Rachel Ruiz   illustrated by Chiara Fedele

PICTURE WINDOW BOOKS
a capstone imprint

The school bell rang. Young Rosa Parks gathered her things and headed home. Halfway there, a white boy on roller skates tried to push her off the sidewalk. Rosa pushed him back.

"I didn't want to be pushed, seeing that I wasn't bothering him at all," she later said.

"I know, child," Rosa's mother said. "But I worry."

In the 1920s, black people were not supposed to push or even talk back to white people. They could be arrested — or worse. Rosa grew up trying to stop the unfair treatment of others. And then one day in 1955, she did something simple and brave. She sat down in a bus seat — and became a hero to millions of people.

Rosa Louise McCauley was born on February 4, 1913, in Tuskegee, Alabama. Her father, James, was a traveling woodworker. Her mother, Leona, was a teacher.

Rosa's mother loved to learn. She passed that love of learning on to Rosa. She also taught Rosa to have respect for herself and others. She said it was the most important thing.

Rosa and her family lived on her grandparents' farm in
Pine Level, Alabama. They had fruit, pecan, and walnut trees.
They also had a garden and raised a few animals.

Rosa enjoyed exploring the nearby woods, ponds, and
creeks with her younger brother, Sylvester. He followed her
everywhere she went and repeated everything she said.

Money was scarce, but Rosa's family found ways to make do with what they had. They didn't buy ready-made clothes. Rosa's mother sewed their clothes. She was a good seamstress. She taught Rosa to sew too.

While their mother worked at the school, Rosa and Sylvester spent time with their grandparents. They fished at the nearby creek. Rosa learned a lot from her grandparents.

"Remember to always stand up for what you believe in, Rosa," Grandma Rose said.

"And don't let people push you around," Grandpa John added.

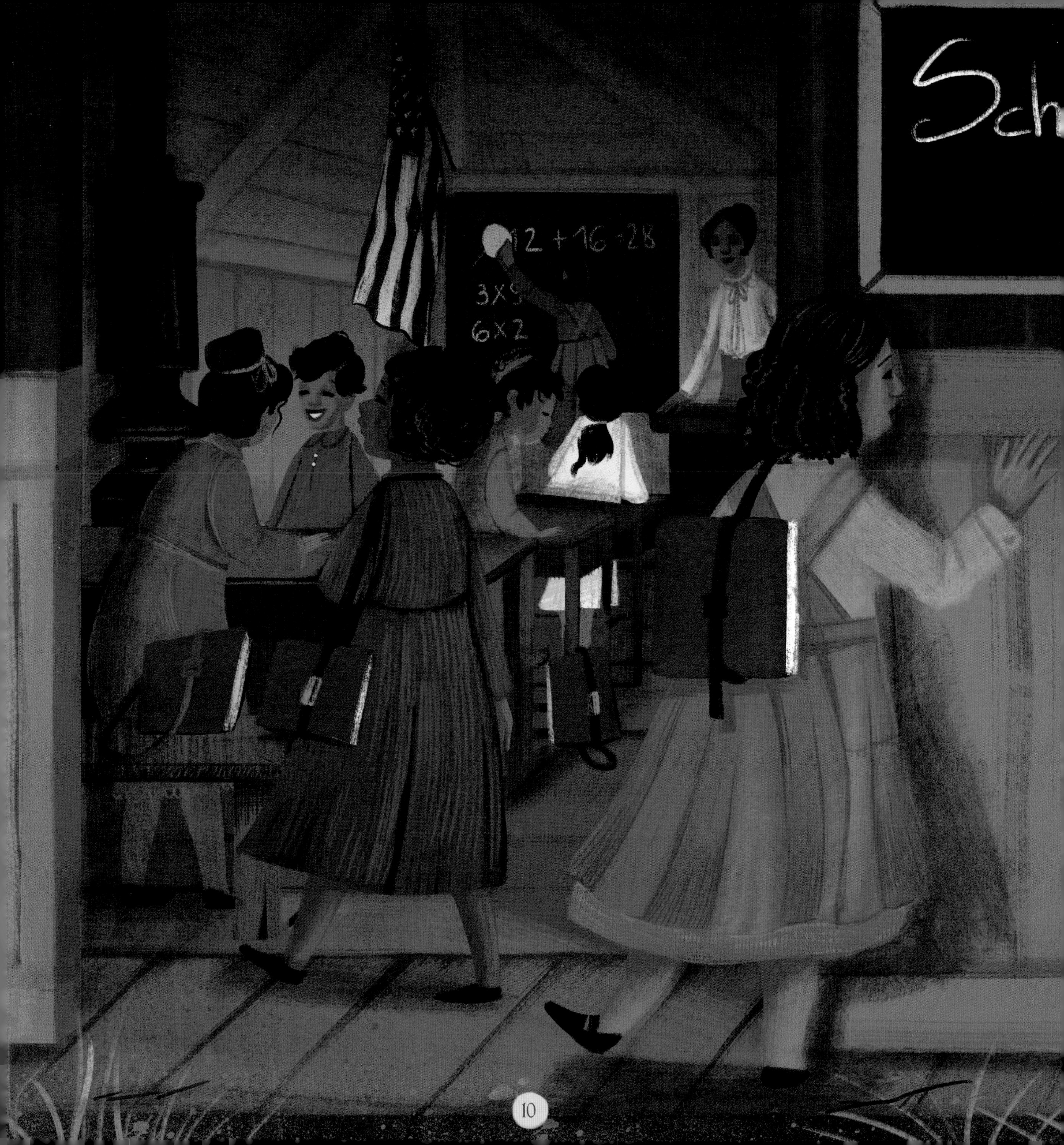
Sch
12 + 16 = 28
3x9
6x2

Rosa started school in 1919, at age 6. She went to an all-black one-room schoolhouse, and she loved it! She already knew how to read. Her mother had taught her since Rosa was just 3 years old.

At recess, Rosa and the other little girls played games. They laughed and sang their way through "Little Sally Walker Sitting in the Saucer" and "Ring Around the Roses."

About this time, Rosa learned a big, hard lesson: Beyond her grandparents' farm, life could be dangerous for black people. There were groups of white people who hated anyone whose skin wasn't white. They burned down black people's homes and churches. Sometimes, white kids called hurtful names. They threw rocks at Rosa and her friends.

Rosa was angry. Why did people act that way? Didn't everyone deserve respect? That's what Rosa's mother had always told her. Didn't blacks deserve to be treated the same as whites?

In the summer of 1921, Rosa's mother took her to Montgomery, Alabama. Eight-year-old Rosa was amazed by the big, modern city. It was much different than Pine Level! Tall buildings stretched up to the sky. Shops selling fancy dresses and hats lined the sidewalks.

Montgomery was the first place Rosa saw segregation. The law said that people could be treated differently because of their skin color. There were separate drinking fountains for white people and black people. The fountains were labeled "White" and "Colored."

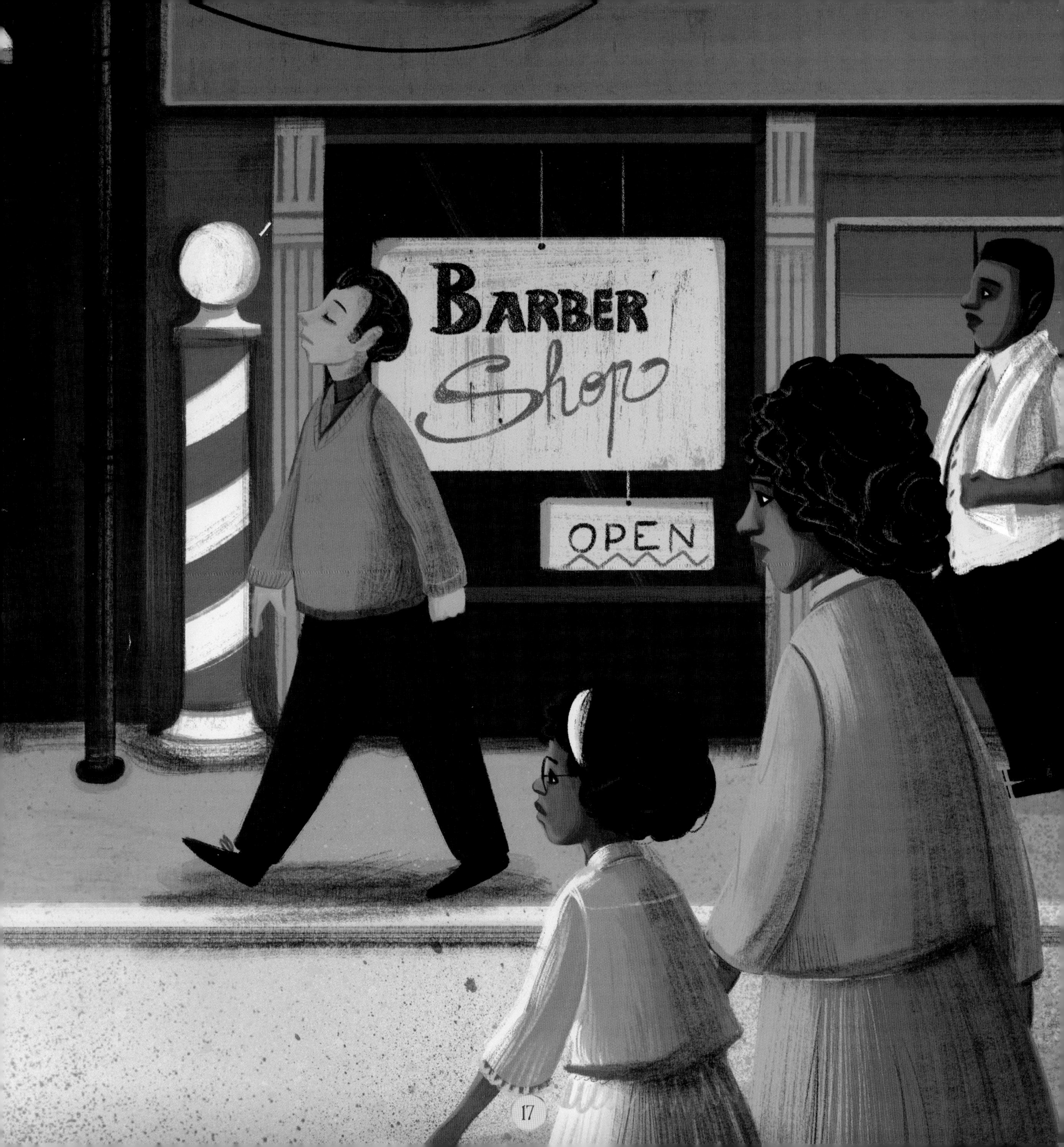
BARBER
Shop
OPEN

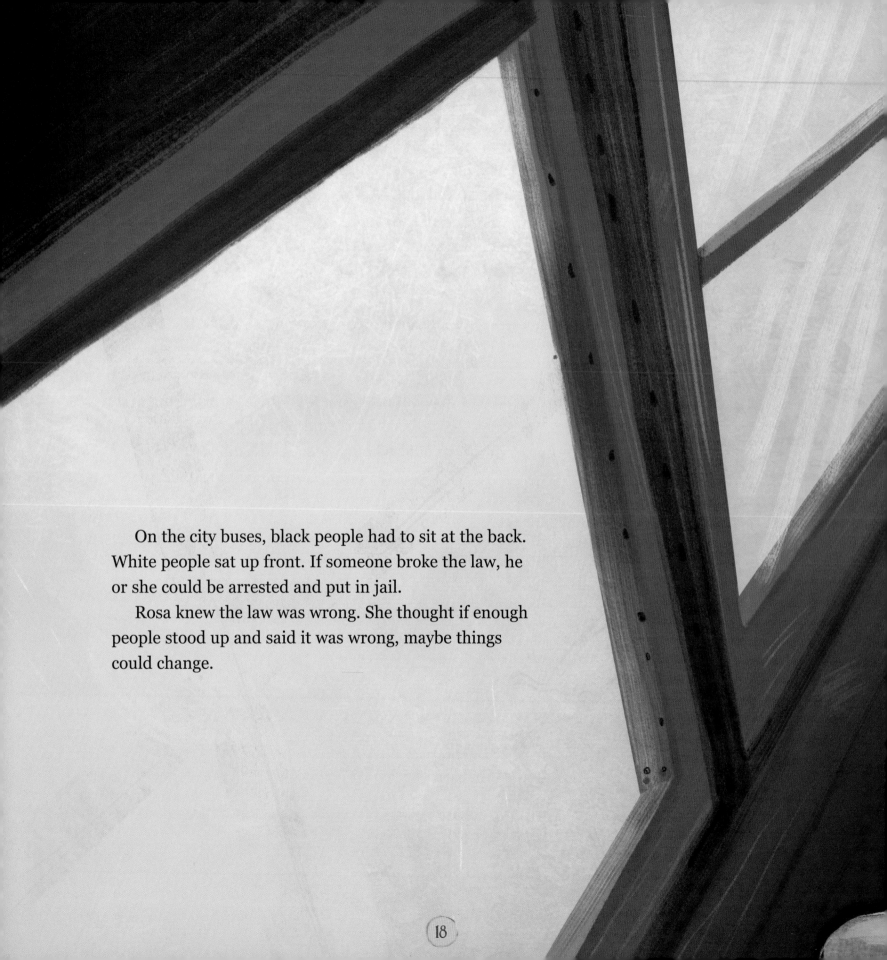

On the city buses, black people had to sit at the back. White people sat up front. If someone broke the law, he or she could be arrested and put in jail.

Rosa knew the law was wrong. She thought if enough people stood up and said it was wrong, maybe things could change.

After she finished fifth grade, Rosa went to live with her aunt Fannie in Montgomery. There were better schooling options in the city for Rosa. She became a student of Montgomery Industrial School for Girls. Everyone called it "Miss White's School." Miss Alice White was the principal and co-founder.

Miss White was Caucasian. So were all the teachers at the school. They had moved there from the Northern states. At the time, black girls in the South had few places to go to school. Miss White and her teachers wanted to change that fact.

Rosa adored Miss White. From her, Rosa learned many lessons. She learned that she was a person who deserved to be treated fairly and equally. She also learned to set high goals for herself.

"Believe anything in life is possible," Miss White said.

Rosa and Miss White wrote letters to each other long after Rosa left school. Rosa treasured their friendship. It reminded her that not all white people hated black people.

When Rosa was 16, she left high school to help care for her ill grandmother. Rosa wasn't happy about leaving school. But she did not complain. Nothing was more important to her than family.

Rosa worked hard cleaning houses to earn money. Sometimes she needed more money, so she sold fruit from her family's trees.

It was a tough time for Rosa. She often looked to her church for help. Her faith got her through many long, hard days.

When Rosa was 18, she met Raymond Parks. They married the following year, in 1932. Like Rosa, Raymond loved learning. He was one of the first members of the National Association for the Advancement of Colored People (NAACP). The organization worked to improve the lives of black people across the nation. Later, Rosa also joined the NAACP.

Rosa was happy. But she always regretted not finishing high school. With Raymond's support, she went back to school. And in 1934, Rosa reached her goal: She earned her high school diploma.

Nearly 20 years later, Rosa would stand up for herself and others in a big way — by taking a seat.

AFTERWORD

On December 1, 1955, Rosa Parks got on a bus to go home. She sat in the black section, like she was supposed to. But when the bus filled up, the bus driver told her to get up and give her seat to a white man. Rosa refused, saying calmly, "No." When the driver said he was going to call the police, Rosa said quietly, "You may do that."

Some people later said that Rosa didn't give up her seat because she was old and tired. "I was 42," she replied. "No, the only tired I was was tired of giving in."

Rosa was arrested and later let out of jail. There was a trial. She was found guilty and told to pay $14. She also lost her job. In protest, thousands of people, mostly black, boycotted the city buses in Montgomery. The boycott lasted more than a year.

Rosa and her lawyer thought the ruling was unfair, so they went to the U.S. Supreme Court. The court ruled on November 13, 1956, that bus segregation in Alabama must end. From then on black people were free to sit wherever they wanted on a bus.

Rosa Parks became an important leader in the civil rights movement in America. She died on October 24, 2005, at age 92.

GLOSSARY

arrested—stopped and held in jail because a law may have been broken

boycott—to stop buying or using a product or service to show support for an idea or group of people

Caucasian—a person who is of white European descent, not of Hispanic origin

civil rights—the rights that all people have to freedom and equal treatment under the law

lawyer—a person who is trained to advise people about the law

NAACP—a civil rights organization founded in 1909; abbreviation for National Association for the Advancement of Colored People

protest—to speak out about something strongly and publicly

regret—to feel sad or disappointed about something, especially something that should've been done differently

respect—to believe in the quality and worth of others and yourself

segregation—the practice of keeping groups of people apart, especially based on skin color

trial—the court process to decide if a charge or claim is true

U.S. Supreme Court—the most powerful court of law in the United States

READ MORE

Hansen, Grace. *Rosa Parks: Activist for Equality*. History Maker Biographies. Minneapolis: Abdo Kids, 2016.

Jazynka, Kitson. *Rosa Parks*. National Geographic Readers. Washington, D.C.: National Geographic, 2015.

Shea, Therese. *Rosa Parks: Heroine of the Civil Rights Movement*. Britannica Beginner Bios. New York: Britannica Education Publishing, in association with Rosen Educational Services, 2015.

CRITICAL THINKING
QUESTIONS

1)   List three childhood character traits or abilities of Rosa Parks. Use facts and illustrations from the book to support your answer.

2)   Name two adults who helped shape young Rosa Parks into the smart, strong leader she became. Explain how they helped, using evidence from the text to support your answers.

3)   As a child, Rosa was pushed by a white boy. As an adult, she was told to give up her bus seat to a white man. Explain how the two events were alike and different. Then explain how Rosa responded to each event.

INTERNET SITES

Use FactHound to find Internet sites related to this book.

Visit *www.facthound.com*

Just type in 9781515815747 and go.

Super-cool stuff!

Check out projects, games, and lots more at
www.capstonekids.com

OTHER TITLES IN THIS SERIES

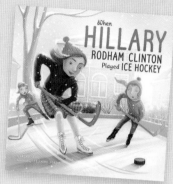
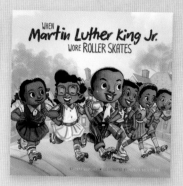

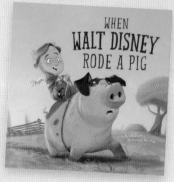

INDEX

boycott, 28

buses, 2, 18, 28

Montgomery, Alabama, 14, 16, 18, 21, 28

Montgomery Industrial School for Girls, 21

NAACP, 26

Parks, Raymond, 26, 27

Parks, Rosa

  birth, 4

  brother, 7, 9

  church, 25

  clothing, 8

  death, 28

  father, 4

  fishing, 9

  grandparents, 7, 9, 12, 24

  home, 7, 12, 14

  life lessons, 4, 9, 12, 22

  marriage, 26

  mother, 2, 4, 8, 9, 11, 14

  school, 11, 21–23, 24, 27

segregation, 16, 18, 28

unfair treatment of others, 2, 12, 16, 18, 28

White, Alice, 21–23

Special thanks to our adviser for his advice and expertise:
Timothy N. Thurber, Professor of History
Virginia Commonwealth University, Richmond, Virginia

Editor: Jill Kalz
Designer: Russell Griesmer
Creative Director: Nathan Gassman
Production Specialist: Katy LaVigne
The illustrations in this book were created digitally.

Editor's Note: Direct quotations in the main text are indicated by **bold** words.
Direct quotations are found on the following pages:
Page 2, lines 4–5: Parks, Rosa, with Jim Haskins. *Rosa Parks: My Story.*
New York: Dial Books, 1992, p. 48.
Page 28, lines 4–5: Ibid, p. 116.
Page 28, lines 7–8: Ibid, 116.

Picture Window Books are published by Capstone, 1710 Roe Crest Drive,
North Mankato, Minnesota 56003
www.mycapstone.com

Library of Congress Cataloging-in-Publication data is available on the Library of Congress website.
ISBN: 978-1-5158-1574-7 (library binding)
ISBN: 978-1-5158-1578-5 (paperback)
ISBN: 978-1-5158-1582-2 (eBook PDF)
Summary: What was the civil rights activist Rosa Parks like as a child? Following young Rosa
from a fishing creek to a one-room schoolhouse, from her wearing homemade clothes to wondering
what "white" water tastes like, this book highlights the early experiences that shaped
one of the most famous African-Americans in history.

Printed and bound in the United States of America.
010363F17